MEDICAID REIMBURSABLE PEER-TO-PEER ENGAGEMENT DOCUMENTATION MANUAL

(RECOVERY COACH/PEER PROVIDER PROFESSIONAL NON-CLINICAL S.O.A.P NOTATION METHODOLOGY)
*NEW YORK STATE OASAS CERTIFIED 8-CEU RENEWAL HOURS COURSE FOR CASAC AND PEER SUPPORT

Lucious Conway
Recovery Coaching Service of New York, LLC

ISBN
ISBN-

"Greater love hath no man than this, that a man lay down his life for his friends."
John 15.13

"A friend loves at all times, And a brother is born for adversity."
Proverbs 17:17

"A man who has friends must himself be friendly, But there is a friend who sticks closer than a brother."
Proverbs 18:24

CONTENTS

1 INTRODUCTION

The Affordable Care Act and its mandate that insurance companies cover people diagnosed with Substance Use Disorder (SUD) (formerly called Addiction) and Serious Mental Illness (SMI) precipitated the continued growth of states seeking ways to use Recovery Coaches/Peer Support providers within the SUD/SMI continuum of care. The challenge that the states have faced have predominately revolved around how to make this role Medicaid reimbursable. The fact that Recovery Coaches/Peer Providers are not, within the language of the Social Security Administration Regulations and state Medicaid Departments, Qualified Health Professionals has prevented Medicaid billing for them. Until now.

In 2013 Lucious Conway, then a Recovery Coach, created Recovery Coaching Service of New York, LLC at the behest of the White House Office of National Drug Control Policy, Recovery Branch Chief, Peter Gaumond. This on the heels of Mr. Conway's creation of the first self-directed, wellness-driven Cognitive Behavioral Health Therapy he named Emotional Dispositional Therapy, codified in his book, "My Daily Alcoholic and Addict P.R.A.H.R" (Prevention, Recovery and Help Ritual).

Mr. Gaumond said to Mr. Conway that he believed Mr. Conway could create a program for the pan-recovery movement that might be replicated nationwide. This pan-recovery movement acknowledged that there are many pathways to recovery, from 12-Step Programs abstinence to Harm Reduction Programs wellness-based modality. Having extensively researched the work of William White and graduated the Connecticut Center for Addiction Recovery 40-Hour Recovery Coach Course, Mr. Conway somehow saw how he could lead the nation in the Medicaid reimbursable provision of the peer support service.

From Mr. White's June 2016 Blog: "The title "recovery coach" and the function of "recovery coaching" are being claimed by people of widely varying education, training, and experience. Though the roots of recovery coaching date to the early nineteenth century, the formalization of this role is a relatively recent development that flows from efforts to increase the recovery orientation of addiction treatment and to increase the relevance of other helping roles to people recovering from alcohol- and other drug-related problems.

...While the summarized evidence suggested considerable promise for this new role, a major barrier to effective evaluation and replication is the lack of clarity of how this role is being defined and practiced.

… Each [role] has the potential to exert optimal, minimal, neutral, or negative effects on recovery initiation and long-term recovery maintenance as well as on other critical outcome measures. Rigorous evaluations of each role help identify "active service ingredients" (those critical dimensions that effect recovery outcomes); define core knowledge, competency requirements, and ethical guidelines; distinguish each role from other professional and lay support roles; and provide a framework for recruitment, orientation, training, and on-going supervision of service delivery.

…Recovery coaches of varied backgrounds are being integrated within addiction treatment organizations and within allied service settings (e.g., primary health care, public health, criminal justice, child welfare). And "professional recovery coaching" is being offered as a service by life coaches, interventionists, and private psychotherapists.

Several years ago, Alida Schuyler, Jan Brown, and I began an extended dialogue (via phone conferences) on recovery coaching and the need for clearer definitions and standards governing this role. Alida drew from her roots in the professional coaching arena. Jan drew from her roots as a professional coach and her knowledge and experience from her work in the development of peer-based recovery support services within recovery community organizations and addiction treatment programs. I drew on my experience as an addictions counselor, clinical supervisor, and on my consultations and evaluations of peer-based recovery support services."

This need for "effective evaluation and replication" was addressed and resolved by Mr. Conway in the solitude of his Harlem, New York residence and recognized by the OMICS International 2nd International Conference and Exhibition on Addiction Research & Therapy July 22-24, 2013 Las Vegas, USA where Mr. Conway was invited to Keynote and Moderate the 3 day conference of addiction psychiatrists, psychologists, medical doctors, and therapists as well as research scientist in the field.

OMICS, and the White House we're not the only ones to recognize Mr. Conway as a subject matter expert as regards recovery coaching and peer support services. In 2015 Mr. Conway was invited by New York State to participate on the exclusive role delineation study panel to name and define the role of Medicaid reimbursable peer support providers within the state. Thus was created the role and title of Certified Recovery Peer Advocates. Mr. Conway had already created Medicaid reimbursable Non-clinical S.O.A.P. Notation Methodology and secured a contract and credentialing from UnirdHealthcare/Optum insurance company as the sole in network Peer Support Provider which position his company still holds since 2014. And holds the same position with Fidelis insurance company since 2017.

Herein his innovative method is made available to you in simple terms. Finally, this method makes it easy to document and guide you in your peer support service delivery. And it is the best Medicaid reimbursable method in the United States. Mr. Conway is a New York State OASAS CERTIFIED EDUCATION AND TRAINING PROVIDER as this course is CCERTIFIED for 8-CEU RENEWAL HOURS for CASAC and Peer Providers in New York.

2 OVERVIEW, PURPOSE AND PROCESS

Slide 1

Best Practices In
Recovery Coach/Peer Advocate
Service Delivery
Documentation
Non-Clinical S.O.A.P. Notation
2015

MODULE 1:
The Conceptual Framework for
Recovery Coach/Peer Advocate Service
Delivery
Documentation
"Non-Clinical S.O.A.P. Notes"

If it is not in writing then it never happened.

My Obligation!

Webinar Facilitator
Lucious Conway, CRPA

Recovery Coaching Service of New York, LLC

Self-Directed, Wellness-Driven Peer Mentors

"If it's not in writing then it never happened", was my first and most important law school lesson. Documentation is essential in life from Birth Certificates to Death Certificates to Divorce Decrees, and Marriage and Business Licenses between. So too, critical is the documentation of peer engagement to prove its' efficacy and worthiness of payment by Behavioral Health Organizations (BHO's). This manual is designed to guide peers engaging peers on the method I created for Medicaid reimbursable documentation of each and all types of encounters. As well as introduce you to Electronic Medical/Health Records (EMR/EHR) platforms where this information may be recorded as well as hardcopy formats utilized.

Slide 2

ABOUT **RECOVERY COACHING SERVICE OF NEW YORK, LLC** **MODULE 1**

My Obligation!

RECOVERY COACHING SERVICE OF NEW YORK, LLS (RCS) is an addiction peer mentoring, support specialist service, weekly wellness planning, self-help motivational seminars and holistic wellness book publishing company. With a corporate office in New York, New York, RCS achieves its business objectives through an extensive international network of dedicated addiction research and therapy independent, government, and corporate behavioral health scholars and practitioners.

RCS HAS FOUR PRACTICE AREAS: (1) Peer Support/Bridger Services; (2) peer to peer documentation training; (3) community engagement and knowledge dissemination; and (4) holistic wellness multi media book publishing.

RCS' MISSION: is to help recoverees/clients/peers (1) develop, (2) implement and (3) maintain the strategy, motivation and accountability required to succeed in living a healthy, successful and independent life, through providing face-to-face, telephone and internet encouragement and support, as well as skill development.

RCS' VISION: is to "model, mentor, and motivate peers to sustained wellness." We do this by demonstrating the positive use of wellness tools and methods or best practices from a pan-recovery perspective. Our individual lives reflect the effective use of these tools in our daily affairs as well as our short and long term goals across at least Seven Dimensions of Wellness our lives encompass.

Self-Directed, Wellness-Driven Peer Mentors

July 17, 2013 when Recovery Coaching Service of New York, LLC was officially created New York State had not yet decided the title or role peers working with other peers with Substance Use Disorder (SUD) and/or Serious Mental Illness (SMI) would take on. But, I had some idea of what that may be. Helping peers develop, implement and maintain strategies is at the core of what RCS is, what our Four practice areas are, what our mission remains and how through vision we practice this program. Doing this without molding the peer into our own image and without influencing the peer on the path of "recovery" (what we at RCS call "life discovery") he or she may or may not choose.

Wellness in life discovery is what we are all about. And a systematic approach is our key.

_____

_____

_____

_____

_____

_____

_____

_____

_____

_____

_____

_____

_____

_____

_____

_____

_____

Slide 3

Dr. Conway, as he is called by Addiction Research and Therapy professionals worldwide is a Behavioral Scientist by divine design. Intrigued with B.F. Skinner and his Behavior Modification theory and tests at the ripe old age of 12 years, Skinner's question of the carrot or the stick and belief that positive reinforcement was more powerful a motivator for behavioral change than punishment rung true to Dr. Conway's ears. And, the study of Maslow and his Hierarchy of Needs and Pavlov's Classical Conditioning Theory further advanced his own experiments in behavior modification conducted on himself and others around him. His classmates in Walter F. White Elementary School nicknamed him "the nutty professor". This is of course when only the Jerry Lewis version existed, and ironically the film was released in June of 1963 when Dr. Conway was only 5 months old. Needless to say it remains one of his favorite movies. And you may imagine Jekyl and Hyde of him that fed his SUD/SMI diagnosis and failed treatment, which occasioned his brainchild creation of Emotional Dispositional Therapy, a self-directed, wellness driven cognitive therapy codified in his book, "My Daily Alcoholic and Addict P.R.A.H.R.

(Prevention, Recovery and Help Ritual). This was the first of his Wellness Books. He has written and published 3 more wellness books since, the first translated into Urdu by Professor Naumana Amjad of University of Punjab in India. Dr. Amjad told Dr. Conway that in her culture his codified experience is more valuable than gold and so is he. She then referred him to his first Skype peer participant. Who today is living a life of wellness, marriage, poetry writing, making music and working without active SUD plaguing his existence. The last time he was in treatment was during his beginning sessions with Dr. Conway (Lucious though he insists on being called). That was in 2013!

Dr. Conway possess no Phd. or M.D. but that hasn't stopped psychiatrist, psychologists, medical doctors and researchers with Phd's from continuing to refer to him as Dr. Conway. And having created a recognized cognitive therapy treatment, perhaps they're right to do so.

Slide 4

THE BUSINESS OF RECOVERY COACHING: BILLING, EFFICACY AND ACCOUNTABILITY THROUGH NON CLINICIAL DOCUMENTATION

A service business is a commercial enterprise that provides work performed in an **expert manner** by an individual or team for the benefit of its customers. The typical service business provides intangible products, such as accounting, banking, consulting, cleaning, landscaping, education, insurance, treatment, and transportation services. And the business of coaching is more like unto consulting with some marked differences. Recovery Coaching and Peer Advocacy for purposes of Medicaid reimbursement anyway, does not include directly advising the participant peer on what if any method or mode of recovery they should take or how, in general, they should live their lives. We ARE NOT life coaches! Our billing justification must support this.

When Certified Recovery Peer Advocates (CRPAs) submit claims for peer to peer face to face engagement the documentation must demonstrate both that the peer provider understands their service role and that the engagement is justified by the progressive wellness outcome of the encounter, otherwise the claim (bill) will not be paid. A lot of CASACs (Credentialed Alcoholism and Substance Abuse Counselors) have become CRPAs and use language learned from their CASAC documentation training to record engagements in their CRPA performance. For example:

S.O.A.P. Note (This should be a Non-Clinical Note)

Subjective

RC met with recoveree on 12/29/16. The reason for the visit was a follow up on weekly contingency plan. Recoveree stated that he wanted to cut down on smoking tobacco. Recoveree stated that his plan was to go down to 5 cigarettes a day. Recoveree stated that he is now down to 2-3 per day. Regarding his social wellness, recoveree stated that he realized he had to be more open-minded to other people's point of view. Recoveree stated that he will **follow the RC's suggestion of attending AA**. Recoveree stated that the last session has been pushing him to the realization that he needs more support. Recoveree stated that for the last week he has been stuck in an ongoing obsession over drug use. Recoveree's drug of choice is meth.

Objective

Recoveree did display some anxiety about the discomfort with his obsession. Recoveree **expressed himself clearly** and **did not display any aggressive behaviors**. Recoveree **did not show any signs of being influence under any mind or mood altering chemical**.

Assessment

Despite his anxiety the recoveree is following through his plans. He stated that he will attend a AA meeting today on 12/29/16 to keep himself away from isolation. Recoveree did state that the isolation is affecting his thought patterns. **RC educated the recoveree of the importance of staying the course through the 5 stages of change. The outcome of the session indicates that the recoveree is on the action phase.**

Plan

Will resume attending AA and will follow the necessary steps needed. Will see his therapist and continue seeing therapist on a weekly basis. Will also continue to attend mutual aid groups at GMHC. Next session will be on 1/2/17

This Note indicates the Recovery Coach/Peer Advocate is traveling far outside his lane (the scope of his practice and area of expertise) as a Certified Recovery Peer Advocate. Why?

The bold portions of the note indicate where the Recovery Coach/Peer Advocate makes statements requiring his own views "about" the peer participant as opposed to the peer's views singularly about himself. We will go into more detail on this note later in the guide and show you how this note should have been written. However, this demonstrates what a CRPA will not be reimbursed for. Perhaps a CASAC could bill for this note but definitely not a CRPA.

Efficacy, defined as the ability to produce a desired or intended result is why the insurance company pays for Medical and Behavioral Health Care. Improvement, no matter how small the increments, is improvement, also called wellness. Here is RCS' specialty. The RCS desired or intended result is noted above. Can you identify it? Yes, healthy, successful living (self-directed, wellness-driven) through developing, implementing and maintaining a systematic strategy, motivation and accountability by the peer participant is the intended result of each encounter. It is the documentation of this "progress" that insurance companies pay for.

Lastly, accountability in the business of CRPA provision, where accountability means the fact or condition of being accountable; responsible can only be demonstrated through documentation. This is why proper documentation is so critical in the provision of CRPA services. It also why the supervision component is so necessary. CRPAs are still humans. And, humans who deal with the challenges of other humans may become overwhelmed and may relapse. I don't mean actually taking a drink or picking up a drug, though that is certainly known to happen. I mean "dry" relapse, where the behaviors of Substance Use Disorder and/or Serious Mental Illness manifest. Weekly check-ins with supervisors allows the CRPA to vent and air any potential issues in service delivery or in their personal life.

Slide 5

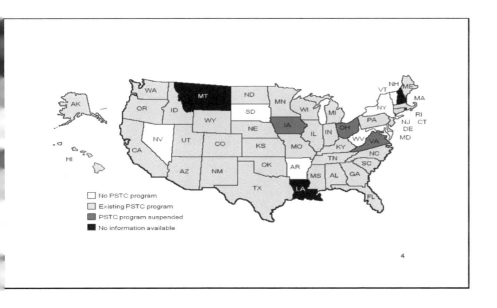

The following is a list of the current Peer workforce throughout the country. However, it is important to note that this is exclusively on the "mental health" side. There are not national numbers for the Substance Use Disorder side. We are the new kids on the block. The pioneers. But you may be sure that our numbers are far, far smaller as are the number of states that have approved us for Medicaid reimbursement.

Most states are using Recovery Coaches without the safeguards of credentialing legally defensible, Medicaid reimbursable Certified Recovery Peer Advocates trained to provide services to both populations diagnosed with Substance Use Disorder and/or Serious Mental Illness. We are breaking ground nationally from New York State through the innovations in the field created by Recovery Coaching Service of New York, LLC. Welcome to the cutting edge you maverick!!!

Peer Specialist Workforce

State-by-state information on key indicators, and links to each state's peer certification program web site.

Alabama

Certification program exists

Peer support not Medicaid-reimbursable

204 peer specialists statewide

www.mh.alabama.gov/MI/consumers.aspx

Alaska

Certification program exists

Peer support Medicaid-reimbursable

Number of peer specialists unknown

www.akpeersupport.org

Arizona

Certification program exists

Peer support Medicaid-reimbursable

2,524 peer specialists statewide

www.azahcccs.gov/shared/Downloads/MedicalPolicyManual/961.pdf

Arkansas

Certification under development

Peer support Medicaid-reimbursable

Number of peer specialists unknown

No web site

California

No certification

Peer support Medicaid-reimbursable

Number of peer specialists unknown

www.dhcs.ca.gov/services/MH/Documents/CMHPCPeerCertPaper.pdf

Colorado

Certification under development

Peer support Medicaid-reimbursable

Number of peer specialists unknown

http://www.coloradomentalwellnessnetwork.org/recovery-education/peer-support-specialist/

Connecticut

Certification program exists

Peer support Medicaid-reimbursable

100 peer specialists statewide

A National Overview of Peer Support Training & Certification Programs

UIC Academy for Policymakers

Delaware

Certification program exists

Peer support Medicaid-reimbursable

29 peer specialists statewide

www.delawarerecovery.org

District of Columbia

Certification program exists

Peer support Medicaid-reimbursable

107 peer specialists statewide

www.dbh.dc.gov/service/peer-specialist-certification-program

Florida

Certification program exists

Peer support Medicaid-reimbursable

421 peer specialists statewide

www.peersupportfl.org

Georgia

Certification program exists

Peer support Medicaid-reimbursable

1700 peer specialists statewide

www.gacps.org

Hawaii

Certification program exists

Peer support Medicaid-reimbursable

190 peer specialists statewide

health.hawaii.gov/amhd/consumer/hcps/

Idaho

Certification program exists

Peer support Medicaid-reimbursable

125 peer specialists statewide

http://healthandwelfare.idaho.gov/Medical/MentalHealth/PeerSpecialists

FamilySupportPartners/tabid/2935/Default.aspx

Illinois

Certification program exists

Peer support Medicaid-reimbursable

359 peer specialists statewide

www.illinoismentalhealthcollaborative.com/consumers/consumer_crss.htm

Indiana

Certification program exists

Peer support Medicaid-reimbursable

378 peer specialists statewide

A National Overview of Peer Support Training & Certification Programs

UIC Academy for Policymakers

Iowa

Certification program exists

Peer support Medicaid-reimbursable

76 peer specialists statewide
http://www.iowabc.org/mhpss
Kansas
Certification program exists
Peer support Medicaid-reimbursable
538 peer specialists statewide
www.webs.wichita.edu/?u=ccsr&p=/certifiedpeerspecialisttraining/
Kentucky
Certification program exists
Peer support Medicaid-reimbursable
556 peer specialists statewide
www.dbhdid.ky.gov/dbh/ebpi-recovery.aspx
Louisiana
Certification program exists
Peer support Medicaid-reimbursable
74 peer specialists statewide
www.lapeersupport.org
Maine
Certification program exists
Peer support Medicaid-reimbursable
100 peer specialists statewide
www.amistadinc.com
Maryland
Certification program exists
Peer support Medicaid-reimbursable
107 peer specialists statewide
http://mapcb.wordpress.com/cprs/
Massachusetts
Certification program exists
Peer support Medicaid-reimbursable
583 peer specialists statewide
transformation-center.org/home/training/certified-peer-specialists/
Michigan
Certification program exists
Peer support Medicaid-reimbursable
1532 peer specialists statewide
www.mpsupeers.org
4 A National Overview of Peer Support Training & Certification Programs
UIC Academy for Policymakers
Minnesota
Certification program exists
Peer support Medicaid-reimbursable
2 peer specialists statewide

www.mentalhealthmn.org/
www.riinternational.com/
Mississippi
Certification program exists
Peer support Medicaid-reimbursable
143 peer specialists statewide
www.dmh.ms.gov/peer-support-services/
Missouri
Certification program exists
Peer support Medicaid-reimbursable
326 peer specialists statewide
www.peerspecialist.org/PeerSpecialist1.0/
Montana
Certification program exists
Peer support Medicaid-reimbursable
Number of peer specialists unknown
www.mtpeernetwork.org
Nebraska
Certification program exists
Peer support Medicaid-reimbursable
320 peer specialists statewide
www.dhhs.ne.gov/behavioral_health/Pages/DBHOCAPeer.aspx
Nevada
Certification under development
Peer support Medicaid-reimbursable
Number of peer specialists unknown
www.NVPPS.com
New Hampshire
Certification program exists
Peer support Medicaid-reimbursable
Number of peer specialists unknown
www.dhhs.nh.gov/dcbcs/bbh/peer.htm
New Jersey
Certification program exists
Peer support Medicaid-reimbursable
34 peer specialists statewide
www.certbd.org/
www.mhanj.org/consumer-connections-2/
A National Overview of Peer Support Training & Certification Programs
UIC Academy for Policymakers
New Mexico
Certification program exists
Peer support Medicaid-reimbursable

362 peer specialists statewide
Web site unknown
New York
Certification program exists
Peer support Medicaid-reimbursable
300 peer specialists statewide
www.nypeerspecialist.org/
North Carolina
Certification program exists
Peer support Medicaid-reimbursable
1834 peer specialists statewide
https://pss.unc.edu/
North Dakota
Certification program exists
Peer support not Medicaid-reimbursable
16 peer specialists statewide
Web site unknown
Ohio
Certification program exists
Peer support Medicaid-reimbursable
Number of peer specialists unknown
www.mha.ohio.gov/Default.aspx?tabid=712
Oklahoma
Certification program exists
Peer support Medicaid-reimbursable
400 peer specialists statewide
www.ok.gov/odmhsas/Mental_Health/Certified_Peer_Recovery_Support_
Specialist/index.html
Oregon
Certification program exists
Peer support Medicaid-reimbursable
515 peer specialists statewide
www.mhaoforegon.org
Pennsylvania
Certification program exists
Peer support Medicaid-reimbursable
4389 peer specialists statewide
www.papsc.org
6 A National Overview of Peer Support Training & Certification Programs
UIC Academy for Policymakers
Rhode Island
Certification program exists
Peer support Medicaid-reimbursable

89 peer specialists statewide
www.ricertboard.org/
South Carolina
Certification program exists
Peer support Medicaid-reimbursable
1000 peer specialists statewide
www.scshare.com
South Dakota
No certification
Peer support not Medicaid-reimbursable
Number of peer specialists unknown
No web site
Tennessee
Certification program exists
Peer support Medicaid-reimbursable
557 peer specialists statewide
www.tn.gov/behavioral-health/topic/certified-peer-recovery-specialist-program
Texas
Certification program exists
Peer support Medicaid-reimbursable
750 peer specialists statewide
www.viahope.org/programs/peer-specialist-training-and-certification/
Utah
Certification program exists
Peer support Medicaid-reimbursable
346 peer specialists statewide
https://dsamh.utah.gov/certified-peer-support-specialist-information-page/
Vermont
Certification program exists
Peer support Medicaid-reimbursable
Number of peer specialists unknown
www.wwcvt.org
Virginia
Certification program exists
Peer support Medicaid-reimbursable
464 peer specialists statewide
https://www.vacertboard.org/certifications
7 A National Overview of Peer Support Training & Certification Programs
UIC Academy for Policymakers
Washington
Certification program exists

Peer support Medicaid-reimbursable
2,500 peer specialists statewide
Web site unknown
West Virginia
Certification program exists
Peer support Medicaid-reimbursable
Number of peer specialists unknown
www.dhhr.wv.gov/bhhf/Sections/programs/ConsumerAffairsCommunity
Outreach/Pages/default.aspx
Wisconsin
Certification program exists
Peer support Medicaid-reimbursable
428 peer specialists statewide
www.wicps.org; www.sce-peerspecialist.uwm.edu
Wyoming
Certification program exists
Peer support Medicaid-reimbursable
56 peer specialists statewide
www.health.wyo.gov/behavioralhealth/mhsa/initiatives/peer-specialists/
Data sources:
Doors to Wellbeing: National Consumer Technical Assistance Center
(2016). Peer Specialists Database. Retrieved from:
https://copelandcenter.com/peer-specialists
Kaufman, L., Kuhn, W., & Stevens Manser, S. (2016). Peer Specialist
Training and Certification Programs: A National Overview. Texas Institute
for Excellence in Mental Health, School of Social Work, University of
Texas at Austin. Visit the Institute's web site here:
http://sites.utexas.edu/mental-health-institute/

Slide 6

While state's certification testing requisites vary across the board there are some consistent requirements:
- Some type of state sanctioned formal training for "Recovery Coaching/Peer Advocacy" and
- Some type of on the job experience with supervision

While pay rates vary as the industry normalizes, New York pays Certified Recovery Peer Advocates $45.50 per 15 minute unit of service. ($92 hourly) downstate New York (within the 5 boroughs). This rate is expected to increase as peer service providers create comprehensive quantitative and qualitative data demonstrating efficacy in cost and outcomes.

DSM 5 (Diagnostic and Statistical Manual of Mental Disorders) codifies SUD and AOD as a mental health (behavioral) disorder of a chronic nature and thus creates the construct for Medicaid and Medicare coverage together with the Parity Act

ICD-10 (International Statistical Classification of Diseases and Related Health Problems) provides codes for billing purposes. Currently peer services fall general under the code H0038

In 2015, as a subject matter expert, Mr. Conway was invited by New York State to participate on the exclusive Florida Certification Board Role Delineation Study panel to name and define the role of Medicaid reimbursable peer support providers within the state. Thus, was created the role and title of Certified Recovery Peer Advocates. As a part of the panel I had the challenge of aiding in the creation of requisite core competencies, domains and tasks each CRPA applicant had to possess in order to sit for the test and passing, receive credentialing.

Currently, Connecticut Community for Addiction Recovery (CCAR)'s 40-hour Recovery Coaching Curriculum is the standard for formal training, along with Recovery Coaching Ethics for those not possessing Ethics training in other disciplines such as a CASAC. This boggles my mind as ethics for a CASAC and a CRPA are drastically different. For example, a CASAC is instructed not to disclose recovery history and a CRPA is; a CASAC is ethically bound to maintain an impersonal difference with his/her "client", a CRPA has no counselor/client relationship it is only peer-to-peer. None-the-less this is the current state of affairs in this burgeoning field. In addition to the formal training (book learning) the potential CRPA must have 500 hours of experience providing peer-to-peer services. And this in almost any capacity including church work, mentoring, etc… and 25 of those hours must be supervised and the agency must provide documentation validating the same. Passing the test, which in 2018 cost about $250 to take in addition to the formal course with costs on average the same amount. We're talking about at least a $500 investment to prepare to test for a CRPA. Bear in mind there is no refund if you do not pass the test.

Having had and designed some of the training you may find my unique view of the CRPA field a definite advantage over those who do not have the benefit of it. There are a three pieces of media that stand out in mind to give you a better idea of what the CRPA in community looks like in practice. What RCS calls "boots on the ground".

First there is the movie "Reign Over Me", the story of a man who lost his wife and two daughters in the 9/11 tragedy and as a consequence, arguably lost himself. It is my belief that as CRPAs and as those diagnosed with Substance Use Disorder and/or Serious Mental Illness, as humans we are subject to lose ourselves because of one event or another, real or imagined. I further, believe that only unconditional love will help us find our way back to the heart of who we are and what our true desire is, believing we can and will achieve it. It is here that my pan-recovery strength-based approach veers from the traditional and failed treatment approach that necessitated the creation of the CRPA role. Peer Support Organizations that talk about "recovery" per say are following a failed path. Wellness is the innovation of the CRPA, not problem centered treatment; you're an addict and if you don't pick up you won't get high or stay away from that first drink.

My fundamental argument with this approach is that it's objective is to put you back where you were before you picked up or took that first drink. If the environment that precipitated the onset or re-activation of your SUD/SMI has not changed, what makes you think you will by returning to it? I contend that the strength-based approach is far stronger and better. Discovery instead of recovery is key. Helping a person not define themselves by Diabetes, AIDs, High Blood Pressure or any other ailment is essential to empowering them to strive for wellness in all areas. The CRPA is not a supplement to treatment or treatment providers, but an aid to the peer participant in securing housing, job, career, education, food or rather his or her dream. It is the agenda of the peer participant that guides the engagement not the objective of anyone else.

In this movie "Reign Over Me" Don Cheadle's character is cast in the role of a peer mentor kind of, trying to restore his friend to wholeness. The friend played by Adam Sandler delights in his company, his friendship. Being with him. Playing a video game, having pizza, going to the movies. These are some of things a CRPA may find him or herself doing with a peer participant. Time and experience have taught me that all too many peers with SUD/SMI are alone or very lonely. Some neither read nor write at 30 years old. Some are without any kind of support at all. No one to call friend. Some are transsexual or transvestites or gays or lesbians or bisexual who have been alienated by who they are from those they love and those who should love them.

The CRPA is not about tolerance, but acceptance. I don't have to understand you to accept you in love. I don't have to agree with your choices but I am obligated to fight for your right to make them. And be there to help you up when you fall. It is through this testing of the CRPAs commitment to the peer participant that trust is developed and the growth of both begins. Don' Cheadle's character though overstepped in suggesting therapy. Motivational Interviewing is how we would come to that and only if the peer participant showed a displeasure with some emotional discomfort they may be experiencing and determined to work on that dimension of wellness (we will address the 7 dimensions of wellness later in this guide).

And then there is "The Spanish Gardner". In "Reign Over Me" it is about friendship without condition or with very broad ones. In "The Spanish Gardner" it is about mentoring; sharing your positive personal experience in life with someone who wants to know it. In this field, in New York State most of the people diagnosed with SUD/SMI who are frequent flyers in hospitals, emergency rooms and rehabs are African American Males 40 +. So being able to relate to such an individual genuinely requires study, patience and honesty with the peer participant. This is also true with the LGBTQ community, Indigenous people, Latins, Asians and others. Knowing an individual's Bio-psycho-socio-economic background is a must for a CRPA to relate in a meaningful way with their peer participant.

The age difference in the gardener and the boy is about 5 or so years. Here the mentor is older. In most scenarios this will not be the case with the CRPA in New York City, so tact is all important in not making the peer participant feel dumb or belittled by a know it all CRPA in recovery for 15 years. The peer participant is far less interested in your recovery than in many cases they are their own increased self-awareness. After numerous failed attempts with recovery as the focus most have lost hope. The wise CRPA understands that by first guiding the peer participant in acknowledging their strengths in the majority of dimensions of wellness in life, they are indeed "weller" and stronger than they may have previously imagined, as the gardener did in encouraging the boy in his strengths despite the boy's father constantly talking about how delicate the boy was.

Therein the heart of CRPA service delivery theory and philosophy live.

Most CRPAs can only know this experience by taking themselves through the paces as there were no CRPAs preceding them to share this experience. So, it is essential the CRPA have continued, weekly experience with the tools we use in practice (the 7 Dimensions of Wellness Assessment, the 5 Stages of Change Tool, the Self-Motivational Interviewing Tool, and the Weekly Contingency Management Plan).

In the movie "The Inn of the Sixth Happiness" (Based on a true story), a British maid saved her meager wages to move to China to be a missionary. The movie wonderfully illustrates Christianity in action and not word alone. In fact, it is important to note that in the movie the missionary NEVER predicated adherence to, or acceptance of her religious beliefs on her aid. Likewise, the CRPA, though perhaps possessing religious beliefs, must NOT seek to proselytize the Peer Recipient. But, do all to help the Peer Recipient pursue wellness as the Peer Recipient perceives it. This is not to say that the CRPA is prohibited from sharing their story of spiritual wellness, be it Christianity, Alcoholics Anonymous, Narcotics Anonymous, Harm Reduction, some other path or none in fact.

A Scene from the 20th Century-Fox Production
"THE INN OF THE SIXTH HAPPINESS"
In CinemaScope   Printed in U.S.A.

It is likely the CRPA will find him or herself in "dirty" places and sometimes even dangerous places, for this where many of our Peer Recipients come from and many still live. It is not heard of to provide services to people who are technically homeless, though they may live inside homeless shelters. And, others in slums. This is one of the main reasons CRPA's must exercise self-care and be part of a program that uses the RCS CRPA Supervisor Program. In this way intellectual, emotional and ethical challenges may be evaluated by someone educated and experienced in addressing and aiding in resolving issues arising therefrom.

The truth of matter is that as a friend, the dedicated CRPA will experience sympathy and/or empathy with a Peer Recipient grieving the loss of familial relationships, active Substance Use Disorder and/or Serious Mental Illness. And, it is imperative to understand this is not an indicator that the CRPA is not ideal for this profession. On the contrary, it is the sympathetic/empathetic CRPA whose authentic concern will nurture the trust relationship required to deliver effective service delivery.

For this ongoing personal experience sharing the CRPA rate of pay continues to increase. And, is expected to continue to rise as data is gathered of the sustained success of the program in keeping peers "stabilized" in community, even in the midst of relapse. At the outset New York State's rate of pay in 2015 was $42.00 hourly or $10.50 per 15-minute unit. As you have noted in the slide above this rate has doubled in 3 years without any meaningful data to support it. But, with a great deal of empirical evidence.

RCS is the first in the state to successfully bill and be paid by Medicaid through insurance companies for the CRPA service and this is directly due to the RCS Non-Clinical SOAP Notation Method. And as the pay rate and billing rationales are moving targets in the field, so too is the supervision practice. Since drug counselors and other clinical disciplines function under very different guidelines, these professionals are ill-equipped to supervise the CRPA in doing anything beyond supplementing their role. And this has been the case necessitating the creation of the CRPA Supervision Role and Training which RCS has created and is in the process of having New York State Credential as it has the RCS Non-Clinical SOAP Notation Method also known as the Peer Engagement Documentation Method.

Noted above, weekly supervision is required by New York State Statute to aid the CRPA in their self-care and the ethical delivery of services to other peers, which is achieved by face to face interview in tandem with CRPA case note review. RCS continues to set the bar for the field and this course remains the CRPA case note standard.

The Diagnostic Statistical Manual (DSM) V changed the way what was formerly categorized as drug abuse or dependence in the DSM IV, was viewed. The American Psychiatric Association (APA) sets the criteria for diagnoses for mental health disorders. The DSM-IV was published in 1994 and the DSM V was published in 2013,19 years later.

During those 19 years the science revealed that what was formerly thought to be drug addiction is actually a mental health disorder now termed Substance Use Disorder (SUD). Thus, the DSM V combines the abuse and dependence criteria into SUD adding craving, cannabis, caffeine withdrawal syndrome, aligning Tobacco Use Disorder criteria with other SUDs. So the diagnoses and treatment modalities remain in flux as the vast majority of Substance Use Disorder clinicians practicing were trained as Drug Addiction Counselors with the former science guiding.
The former science basically treated most all SUDs as choice-based addictions. The new science is based on a brain disorder-based illness that must be treated in a different way. So, Medication Assisted Treatment (MAT) modalities has and continues to expand beyond Methadone to include, Naltrexone (Vivitrol), Acamprosate (Campral), and Disulfiram (Antabuse) for Alcohol SUD. For Heroine and Opiate SUD Methodone, Buprenorphine (Suboxone), and Naltrexone are used.

MAT is always used in tandem with some form of clinical counseling and/or peer support. In addition, science has shown that peer support like 12 step programs with their sponsors have been more effective at aiding an individual diagnosed with SUD than clinical treatment methods. And, with this the federal and state governments are seeking out ways to use some version of Recovery Coaches in community to stabilize SUD diagnosed individuals. It is here that RCS remains on the cutting edge, the nations first and currently ONLY non-clinical Peer Support organization authorized to bill Medicaid and Medicare directly!

ICD 10

In billing the ICD-10 Code is provided on clinical documentation for a health insurance participant and is used to substantiate SUD and/or SMI diagnoses. The peer provider transfers this code to peer program files and for insurance coverage and approval of peer support for their member. However, the peer service provider uses the Healthcare Common Procedure Coding System (HCPCS) to bill for 15-minute time increments (called a unit) for peer services (with a minimum of 2 units of service or 30 minutes of service provided). Currently, in 2018 the rate of pay for Downstate HARP (Health and Recovery Plan) BH (Behavioral Health) HCBS (Home and Community Based Services) Medicaid reimbursable peer support services in New York State (as Medicaid is a state program, each state sets their own rates) is $23.80 per unit (15 minutes) or $95.20 per hour.

It is important that the CRPA be aware of this should the agency for whom he or she works, require claims be filed by the CRPA. It is also advantageous for the many agencies that are unfamiliar with billing for this CRPA service, which currently is most of them nationwide.

_____

_____

_____

_____

_____

_____

_____

_____

_____

_____

_____

_____

_____

_____

_____

_____

_____

Slide 7

WHAT TOOLS TO USE

Taking notes is predicated on the type of service you are providing. While changing a car transmission may require some delicacy, open brain surgery probably requires a bit more. Non-clinicians engaging peoples brains (behavior) is like brain surgery in the sense that you are aiding them in developing new ways of thinking that will result in new ways of acting and responding to their internal and external worlds. What tools should you use?

What traditional tools are used in aiding people develop and maintain new ways of thinking that will result in new ways of acting and responding to their internal and external worlds? The clinical tools of drug and alcohol counselors is commonly known as the Individual Service Plan.

Now back to DOCUMENTATION. Remember at the top of slide 4 earlier in this manual. We talked about clinical and non-clinical documentation. This manual is the nations first and currently only Medicaid reimbursable non-clinical documentation method. Which method does not employ peer provider perspectives as does CASAC documentation.

The most important note here is that we do not use the ISP tool. We use the Seven Dimensions of Wellness Self-Assessment Tool, the 5 Stages of Change Tool, the Self-Motivational Interviewing Tool and finally the Weekly Contingency Management Plan Tool. All of these tools are guided by the peer provider sharing his or her experience using the tools and how they work and then documenting the peer service recipient's response to each tool in turn and thus the SOAP Note is created.

_____

_____

_____

_____

_____

_____

_____

_____

_____

_____

_____

_____

_____

_____

_____

_____

_____

_____

_____

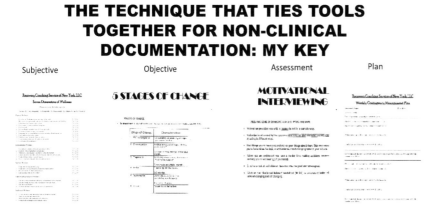

Slide 8

Recovery Coaching Service of New York, LLC

Seven Dimensions of Wellness

Please rate using the following scale

Always (5), Very Frequently (4), Frequently (3), Occasionally (2), Almost Never (1), Never (0)

Physical Wellness

1. I exercise for 20 minutes or more most days of the week.
2. My exercise program includes activities that build my heart, muscles and flexibility.
3. I select lean cuts of meat, poultry or fish
4. I eat a variety of food from all the food groups
5. I eat breakfast
6. I get an adequate amount of sleep (7-8 hours per night)
7. I examine my breasts or testes once a month
8. I participate in recommended routine health screenings (blood pressure, etc.)
9. I seek medical advice when needed
10. I drink less than 5 alcoholic drinks at a sitting
11. I avoid cooking while under the influence of alcohol
12. I avoid using tobacco products

Environmental Wellness

1. I minimize my exposure to second hand tobacco smoke
2. I keep my vehicle maintained to ensure safety
3. When I see a safety hazard, I take steps to correct the problem
4. I choose an environment that is free of excessive noise whenever possible
5. I make efforts to reduce, reuse and recycle
6. I try to create an environment that maximizes my stress

Spiritual Wellness

1. I make time for relaxation in my day
2. I make time in my day for prayer, meditation or personal time
3. My values guide my actions and decisions
4. I am accepting of the views of others

Emotional/Psychological Wellness

1. I am able to sleep soundly throughout the night and wake feeling refreshed
2. I am able to make decisions with a minimum of stress and worry
3. I am able to set priorities
4. I maintain a balance between school, work and personal life

Intellectual Wellness

1. It is easy for me to apply knowledge from one situation to another
2. I enjoy the amount and variety I need
3. I find life intellectually challenging and stimulating
4. I obtain health information from reputable sources

Ben Zimmer in the New York Times 4/16/2010 edition noted, "**Wellness** is generally used to mean a state beyond absence of illness but rather aims to optimize **well-being**." In 2016 the United States Substance Abuse and Mental Health Services Administration (SAMHSA) formally adopted the "8 Dimensions of Wellness" as part of its programs to employ in their "pan-recovery" movement. This movement is based on science and belief that there are many pathways to recovery, from abstinence to harm reduction and every method in between. While SAMHSA defined wellness as having eight aspects: emotional, environmental, financial, intellectual, occupational, physical, social, and spiritual, RCS uses only 7, (**Social Wellness** is the ability to relate to and connect with other people in our world. Our ability to establish and maintain positive relationships with family, friends and co-workers contributes to our Social Wellness.

- **Emotional Wellness** is the ability to understand ourselves and cope with the challenges life can bring. The ability to acknowledge and share feelings of anger, fear, sadness or stress; hope, love, joy and happiness in a productive manner contributes to our Emotional Wellness.

- **Spiritual Wellness** is the ability to establish peace and harmony in our lives. The ability to develop congruency between values and actions and to realize a common purpose that binds creation together contributes to our Spiritual Wellness.

- **Environmental Wellness** is the ability to recognize our own responsibility for the quality of the air, the water and the land that surrounds us. The ability to make a positive impact on the quality of our environment, be it our homes, our communities or our planet contributes to our Environmental Wellness.

- **Occupational Wellness** is the ability to get personal fulfillment from our jobs or our chosen career fields while still maintaining balance in our lives. Our desire to contribute in our careers to make a positive impact on the organizations we work in and to society as a whole leads to Occupational Wellness.

- **Intellectual Wellness** is the ability to open our minds to new ideas and experiences that can be applied to personal decisions, group interaction and community betterment. The desire to learn new concepts, improve skills and seek challenges in pursuit of lifelong learning contributes to our Intellectual Wellness.

- **Physical Wellness** is the ability to maintain a healthy quality of life that allows us to get through our daily activities without undue fatigue or physical stress. The ability to recognize that our behaviors have a significant impact on our wellness and adopting healthful habits (routine checkups, a balanced diet, exercise, etc.) while avoiding destructive habits (tobacco, drugs, alcohol, etc.) will lead to optimal Physical Wellness.

RCS does not use Financial Wellness because we believe that in addressing Occupational and Intellectual Wellness we address Financial Wellness. This self-assessment tool was introduced to me in the CCAR Recovery Coaching Academy Course. Being able to finally realize my life was like a diamond with facets was quite the revelation! It helped me more clearly identify where my Substance Use Disorder and Serious Mental Illness were more likely to become active. In what area of my life was I the least well? And, more importantly what area of my life was I most interested in becoming more well?

In Peer Support Service Delivery, we introduce Peer Support Service Recipients to this tool first and document their engagement with it. This is the Subjective portion of our Non-Clinical SOAP Note. This is why it is requisite that our Certified Recovery Peer Advocates personally engage this tool weekly. The tool is also used in CRPA Supervision and Performance Evaluation. A quote attributed to Civil Rights Legend, Rev. Jesse Jackson, states, "You can't Teach what you don't know, and You Can't Lead where you won't go!" Our job as CRPAs is not to counsel, tell or advise peers what we think they should do, that's left to clinicians. Our CRPA role is to introduce peers to the tools we use, share how they help us find wellness and help them use the tool to find the wellness they want. Our program is Person-Centered, Wellness-Based. And, that in a completely subjective sense. It's about the peers' perceptions, goals and values, not on the CRPA's "educated opinion."

If any, it is this tool that would prove most challenging for the peer recipient, as it may be considered dense with the verbiage and rating scale. So, the CRPA always asks the Peer Participant if they want to read the form or if they want the form read to them. In this way I have often suspected that the Peer Participant cannot read or cannot read and/or comprehend at the level of the language on the form. While we would never confront or even ask the question regarding the person's ability to read, we would discover this fact through the Participants' freely given disclosures. Which disclosures are always predicated on a relationship of trust between the CRPA and the Participant. This trust is only developed over time through the creation, development and maintenance of a genuine FRIENDSHIP between CRPA and Participant. Not above, not beneath, the CRPA walks BESIDE the Participant.

The Five Stages of Change

STAGES OF CHANGE
• In treatment or out of treatment change occurs in stages (see below and #-2.0).

Stage of Change	Characteristics
1. Pre-contemplation	Not currently considering change: "Ignorance is bliss".
2. Contemplation	Ambivalent about change: "Sitting on the fence". Not considering change in the next month.
3. Preparation	Some experience trying to change: "Testing the waters". Planning to act within 1 month.
4. Action	Practicing new behavior. 3-6 months.
5. Maintenance	Continued commitment to sustaining new behavior. 6 months - 5 years.
6. Relapse	Return to old behaviors.

After the Peer Participant

has decided what area (dimension) of Wellness they want to improve we use this tool. The Peer then decides which Stage of Change they are in (how ready they are to make the change they want. Because they have decided to make a

change they are not in the **Pre-Contemplation (ambivalent)** Stage. They have determined that they want to change and can possibly do so. This is the **Contemplation** Stage of Change.

If the peer is convinced that they are in the **Preparation** Stage of Change, they have already done some research on the change. Such as, if they are seeking Environmental Wellness and believe a change of residence is necessary, they have begun to investigate where they might move, what financial challenges they might face, etc. It is important to note that this is not actually going to see people or places or people regarding the move. That would be the **Action** Stage of Change.

In **Action** the Peer is following the plan they created in **Preparation**. And, because all change is task driven, this is not numerous actions each week, but one task (like one phone call or one housing interview). This is to prevent the Peer becoming overwhelmed by the anticipated change. Again, at RCS we eat elephants one bite at a time. An entire slice may be too much. If more is accomplished after the weekly task that is fine. But, it should never be stressed or mentioned by the CRPA. The Peer drives their wellness. Once Action in the same area of wellness is sustained at least 2 weeks, with the 7 Dimensions of Wellness Assessment being administered weekly, and the Peer identifies the same area of wellness in which he/she is working on, the Stage of Change shifts to the next progressive one. In the example above, the Peer will likely identify the **Maintenance** Stage of Change, as where they are.

This brings us to the next tool. **The Self-Motivation Interviewing Tool.**

PROS AND CONS OF CHANGING AND OF STAYING THE SAME

- Motivation provides you with a reason to act in a certain way.

- Motivation is influenced by how you view what you will gain and what you will lose by acting in different ways.

- Most things you do have good and not-so-good things about them. This may cause you to have mixed feelings, or ambivalence, about changing some of your actions.

- When you are ambivalent you have a harder time making decisions because nothing you do will meet all of your needs.

- It helps to look at both sides at the same time, the good and not-so-good.

- Work on the "Decisional Balance" worksheet (W-5.0) to understand better all sides of changing and not changing.

With this tool the Peer weighs the pros and the cons of his/her anticipated change. What If... I do? What if... I don't. Here the adage applies; "If you want what you have, keep doing what you've done." Brainstorming within oneself in the presence of a CRPA "Mentor" helps the Peer be open and honest with themselves, even expressing their fears.

Usually, past failure in an area of attempted change (mostly not being able to sustain "recovery") causes a Peer to be apprehensive about attempting change in any other area. However, the CRPA is there to affirm the sin is not in failing but not trying. At RCS we believe quitters never win and winners never quit. Additionally, this is one of the main reasons the CRPA is there. Many times, all a Peer needs is an ear to bend, a shoulder cry on and a friend to believe in them with them.

Recovery Coaching Service of New York LLC

Weekly Contingency Management Plan

To aid in managing change, RCS utilizes the **Weekly Contingency Management Plan.** One weekly task toward change is all that is targeted. Too often Peers are overwhelmed trying to take on too much change at once. RCS knows that elephants may be eaten... one bite at a time.

The WCMP is about taking one bite of cake weekly. It's not about eating the cake whole, half or by the slice. Sometimes, the Peer's enthusiasm will drive them to complete more than one task in a week toward their change goal. But, CRPA's must be cautious in encouraging this practice as it's sustainability is often challenging beyond a Peers capacity.

Remember this method is a new way of approaching life and wellness goals. And, more than anything sustaining the change method is far healthier than sustaining any single wellness goal. Mastering the technique is wellness in and of itself. Understanding the reality that like the CRPA him or herself, the Peer may not be successful in each area attempted at the offset or may switch the area of change before achieving one started.

This is not a bad thing and should not be perceived as one. If a Peer is working on improving their **Physical Wellness** and is targeting quitting smoking cigarettes and moves from **Contemplation** in week one to **Preparation** in week two and then suddenly has a fire in their home and must relocate, chances are the area of change will rightfully shift to **Environmental Wellness**.
It is the approach to change that makes life challenges manageable and reinforces the strength within the Peer, formerly hidden.

This flexibility in the tools is what makes them so dynamic and powerful. Remember, "relapse does not mean rehab." The non-judgmental, reassuring friendship of the CRPA coupled with the strength affirming reinforcement of the tools correctly used continues to sustain Peer Participants "in community."

MODULE A REVIEW

1) What Federal law mandates insurance companies cover Substance Use Disorder (SUD) and Serious Mental Illness (SMI)?

2) What is the common title used for peer support nationwide?

3) How many New York State OASAS renewal CEUs are granted by completing this course?

4) What is the goal of this manual?

5) RCS employs what systematic approach?

6) What makes a service business?

7) What are Recovery Coaches and Peer Advocates not?

8) What is submitted for Certified Recovery Peer Advocate payments?

9) How are claims justified?

10) When is a Recovery Coach/Peer Advocate functioning outside the scope of his/her practice?

11) What one thing are insurance companies seeking in Peer Advocate peer support?

12) How is accountability demonstrated?

13) What are the national statistics for Substance Use Disorder Peer Advocates?

MODULE 1
BEHAVIORAL HEALTH/ELECTRONIC MEDICAL RECORD (EMR)/CRPA ELECTRONIC PLATFORM WORKFLOW

RCS

HCBS Workflow Reference Guide

Login

User ID:	
Password:	
Organization ID:	rcs
	Log On

Search Participant

Participant Search	Profile
Select Participant	

Register/Create New Participant

- If "No Results Found"
- Then Create New Client
- Complete (at least) all fields with *
- Save

Referral

- Click on New Referral
- Complete Referral information
- Complete Referral into Program

Referral 1

Programs		Site	
HCBS Active	▾	Select One ▾	
Status		**Waitlisted**	**Decision Date**
Accepted	▾	Select One ▾	02-Oct-2017

Save

Insurance

- Create New

This part of the CRPA role may be the most challenging for those who are documentation averse. However, approaching notation creatively will help keep it engaging and enjoyable. As RCS was in front of the curve using the Practice Fusion

When I am afraid, I will direct my attention to being my healthiest me. When any unhealthy dimension of life becomes clear to me, I will work on that dimension of life.

I have the strength to be and do better.

I am grateful to learn about wellness and work on, and become healthier in every dimension of my life with the help of my wellness team.

I let go of all my unhealthy habits and replace them with healthy ones so my will and purpose for my total wellness is fulfilled.

I now strengthen my character making me a positive influence in my life and the lives of those around me.

I have and continuously gain the knowledge, understanding, wisdom and courage to do the right thing as I see it, without fear.

I consult with my wellness team before I take any unhealthy actions that may cause harm to myself or others.

I have and will keep and refine my tools for patience, tolerance, kindliness and love and to live an emotionally healthy life.

I will discuss the urge to take negative actions immediately with at least one member of my wellness team.

7 MY EVENING PRAYERS, AFFIRMATIONS AND MEDITATIONS

Let me be aware of my true self as I review this day.
Was I bitter?

Was I selfish?

Was I dishonest?

Was I afraid?

Do I owe anyone an apology including me?

Did I neglect discussing something with another person immediately?

Was I kind and loving toward everyone?

What could I have done better?

Was I thinking of myself most of the time?

Was I thinking of what I could do for others?

I must make these affirmations true for me.
I will not worry.

I forgive my shortcomings.

I will find what corrective measures to take.

8 THE WELLNESS MEETING MATERIALS

SAMPLE MEETING FORMAT:

1) HI! MY NAME IS _____
2) WELCOME TO ANYONE WHO IS A NEWCOMER.
3) REVIEW GROUP GUIDELINES
4) PLEASE JOIN ME IN A MOMENT OF SILENCE TO REFLECT ON WHY WE ARE HERE AND ON THOSE WHO DO NOT KNOW HOW WELL THEY ARE.
5) PLEASE JOIN ME IN RECITING THE **WILD WELLNESS PLEDGE**
6) WOULD SOMEONE PLEASE READ **WHO IS WELL?**
7) WOULD SOMEONE PLEASE READ **WHAT IS THE WILD PROGRAM?**
8) WOULD SOMEONE PLEASE READ **WHY ARE WE HERE?**
9) **WOULD SOMEONE PLEASE READ HOW IT WORKS?**
10) WOULD SOMEONE PLEASE READ FROM THE BOOK **"IN THIS MOMENT"**

AFTER EVERYONE SHARES THEN WE CAN
READ:

1) TRY TO READ YOU AND DO YOUR **WILD WORKOUT** DAILY AND MEET WITH YOUR ADVOCATE AT LEAST WEEKLY.

2) CONNECT WITH PEOPLE WHO UNDERSTAND, APPRECIATE AND ARE LIVING WELLNESS BASED LIFESTYLES AND MAINTAIN THOSE CONNECTIONS.

3) BUILD YOUR RECOVERY CAPITAL AND KEEP IT FRESH. STAY IN TOUCH WITH YOUR WELLNESS TEAM

4) WOULD SOMEONE PLEASE READ **"IN THIS MOMENT"**

5) CLOSE WITH **WILD WELLNESS PLEDGE**

GROUP RULES
1. BE ON TIME

2. TRY TO REMAIN SEATED DURING GROUP

3. USE "I" STATEMENTS AS OFTEN AS
   POSSIBLE

4. AVOID SPEAKING WHILE SOMEONE ELSE
   IS SHARING

5. PLEASE SPEAK RESPECTFULLY TO YOUR
   PEERS

6. PLEASE USE APPROPRIATE LANGUAGE

W.I.L.D. WELLNESS PLEDGE

I WILL CONTINUALLY WORK TO:

1. MAINTAIN A HEALTHY DIET AND KEEP PHYSICALLY FIT
2. FIND, KEEP AND BE A POSITIVE FRIEND, SELF-DIRECTED AND WELLNESS-DRIVEN
3. NURTURE THE INNER SPARK WHICH IS MY SPIRIT, THE ULTIMATE FORCE DRIVING ME
4. FIND, AND KEEP WORK THAT I LOVE
5. CREATE AND MAINTAIN A SAFE, CLEAN, COMFORTABLE PLACE TO LIVE
6. FIND AND MAINTAIN A HEALTHY EMOTIONAL AND PSYCHOLOGICAL DISPOSITION
7. EXPAND MY MIND BY LEARNING POSITIVE INFORMATION THAT WILL EMPOWER AND ENHANCE MY QUALITY OF LIFE.

WHO IS WELL?

THOSE OF US WHO FEEL IN CONTROL OF OUR
INTELLECTUAL, PHYSICAL, SPIRITUAL, SOCIAL,
ENVIRONMENTAL, EMOTIONAL, AND/OR
OCCUPATIONAL HEALTH ARE WELL. EVEN
THOUGH WE MAY NOT BE 100%. WE ARE WELL
TO SOME DEGREE WHEN WE HAVE A SAFETY
NET IN ANY ONE OR MORE OF THESE 7 AREAS
OF LIFE. WE ARE WELL WHEN WE SET AND
WORK TOWARD GOALS IN ANY OF THESE
AREAS NO MATTER HOW SMALL. WE ARE WELL
WHEN WE ARE FREE TO DO WHAT MAKES US
HAPPY IN ANY OF THESE AREAS.
A WELL PERSON IS ANY PERSON WHO ACTIVELY
SEEKS OPTIMAL WELLNESS IN THESE 7 AREAS
OF LIFE.

WHAT IS THE W.I.L.D. (WELLNESS IN LIFE DISCOVERY) PROGRAM?

WILD IS A FAMILY OF MEN AND WOMEN FOR WHOM WELLNESS HAS BECOME A MAJOR NEED. WE ARE DISCOVERING NEW THINGS ABOUT OURSELVES AND LIFE. WE MEET REGULARLY TO HELP EACH OTHER STAY WELL. THIS IS A PROGRAM OF COMMITMENT TO WELLNESS AND LIVING OUR BEST LIFE. THERE IS ONLY ONE REQUIREMENT FOR MEMBERSHIP: THE DESIRE TO LIVE WELL. WE SUGGEST THAT YOU KEEP AN OPEN MIND AND BELIEVE IN YOURSELF. OUR PROGRAM IS A SET OF TOOL-BASED PRACTICES SO SIMPLE THAT WE CAN USE THEM IN OUR DAILY LIVES. THE MOST IMPORTANT THING ABOUT THEM IS THAT THESE TOOLS WORK.

THERE ARE NO STRINGS ATTACHED TO WILD. WE ARE NOT AFFILIATED WITH ANY OTHER ORGANIZATIONS. WE HAVE NO INITIATION FEES OR DUES, NO PLEDGES TO SIGN, NO

PROMISES TO MAKE TO ANYONE. WE ARE NOT CONNECTED WITH ANY POLITICAL, RELIGIOUS, OR LAW ENFORCEMENT GROUPS. ANYONE MAY JOIN US REGARDLESS OF AGE, RACE, SEXUAL IDENTITY, CREED, RELIGION, OR LACK OF RELIGION.
WE ARE INTERESTED ONLY IN WHAT AREA OF LIFE YOU ARE WORKING ON WELLNESS IN AND HOW WE MAY HELP. THERE ARE NO BIG "I'S" OR LITTLE "U'S" HERE. WE ARE ALL IMPORTANT AND EQUAL. WE HAVE LEARNED FROM OUR INDIVIDUAL AND GROUP EXPERIENCE THAT THOSE WHO USE THESE TOOLS AND PRACTICE WELLNESS REGULARLY IMPROVE IN THEIR OVERALL WELLNESS AND QUALITY OF LIFE.

WHY ARE WE HERE?

WE ARE HERE BECAUSE WE ARE WELL PEOPLE ACTIVELY SEEKING OPTIMAL WELLNESS IN ALL 7 AREAS OF LIFE. TO THIS END WE INVOLVE OURSELVES IN WELLNESS LIVING BY COMING TOGETHER. WE ARE HERE TO FOSTER THE CREATION AND RE-ENFORCEMENT OF PRACTICES ASSOCIATED WITH A WELLNESS LIFESTYLE. BEING HERE TOGETHER HELPS ELEIMANATE COMPULSIVE ACTION AND EXERCISE CONSEQUENTIAL THINKING.

WE RECOGNIZE THE NEED FOR OTHERS LIVING WELLNESS LIFESTYLES AROUND US TO PROVOKE AND ENCOURAGE OUR OWN. HERE WE LISTEN TO AND LEARN FROM EACH PERSON WITH A WELLNESS STRATEGY. AND, WE ARE ABLE TO FOLLOW THE SUCCESS OF OTHERS IN LIVING A SELF-DIRECTED, WELLNESS-DRIVEN LIFE. AS WELL AS SHARE THE BENEFITS OF OUR OWN WELLNESS WITH OTHERS. AND, FINALLY

TO DEVELOP AND MAINTAIN AN ACTIVE LIST OF WELLNESS INFORMED PEOPLE TO KEEP WITH US AT ALL TIMES.

HOW IT WORKS

CONSISTENT USE OF THE **4 TOOLS OF WELLNESS IN LIFE DISCOVERY** MAKE OPTIMAL WELLNESS IN LIVING PRACTICAL, POSSIBLE AND PROBABLE.

1) **THE WELLNESS ASSESSMENT TOOL** HELPS US IDENTIF THE 7 AREAS OF LIFE AND HOW WELL WE ARE IN EACH. ONCE IDENTIFIED, WE MAY THEN DECIDE WHICH SPECIFIC AREA OF OUR LIFE WE WILL IMPROVE.

2) **THE 5 STAGES OF CHANGE TOOL** IS USE SO WE KNOW WHERE WE ARE IN TERMS OF WHICH STATE OF OR ATTITUDE TOWARD POSITIVE CHANGE WE ARE IN REGARDING THE AREA OF LIFE WE HAVE CHOSEN TO CHANGE IN. AS WELL AS TO KNOW THE NEXT STAGE OF CHANGE WE MUST MOVE TO IN ORDER TO PROGRESS

IN OUR GOAL TO POSITIVELY CHANGE IN THE AREA WE HAVE CHOSEN.

3) **THE SELF-DIRECTED MOTIVATIONAL INTERVIEWING TOOL** IS USED TO HELP US REFLECT ON THE AREA OF WELLNESS AND STAGE OF CHANGE WE HAVE CHOSEN AND ARE IN, SO WE MAY DEVELOP A STRATEGY BY WHICH WE MAY MOVE TO THE NEXT STAGE OF CHANGE IN THE AREA OF LIFE WE'VE CHOSEN TO WORK ON.

4) **THE WEEKLY CONTINGENCY MANAGEMENT PLAN TOOL** IS USED TO DOCUMENT THE OVERALL WELLNESS GOAL IN A SPECIFIC AREA OF LIFE AND DOCUMENT SMALL WEEKLY TASK TO ACHIEVE SHORT TERM GOALS THAT WILL LEAD TO THE ULTIMATE LONG TERM GOAL.

WE USE THESE FOUR TOOLS WITH THE HELP OF ONE OR MORE OTHERS BEGINNING WITH A CERTIFIED RECOVERY PEER ADVOCATE AND

MEMBERS OF A W.I.L.D. SUPPORT GROUP
MEETING.
WE BELIEVE THAT EVEN W.I.L.D. DREAMS DO
COME TRUE WHEN APPROACHED SIMPLY AND
SYSTEMATICALLY WITH THE HELP OF OTHERS.
WE SEE WELLNESS IN OUR LIVES AND FOCUS
OUR ATTENTION ON ITS' MAINTENANCE,
ENHANCEMENT AND ENLARGEMENT, ONE
SIMPLE TASK AT A TIME.

IN THIS MOMENT

IN THIS MOMENT, I WILL TREAT OTHERS AS I WANT TO BE TREATED.

IN THIS MOMENT, I WILL DO POSITIVE THINGS THAT BRING POSITIVE THOUGHTS, WHICH BRING POSITIVE FEELINGS.

IN THIS MOMENT, I WILL BE DECISIVE ABOUT BEING AND STAYING WELL AND WHOLE.

IN THIS MOMENT, I UNDERSTAND I HAVE A GIFT WHICH IS MY OPPORTUNITY TO CHOOSE TO LIVE WELL.

IN THIS MOMENT, I CHOOSE TO BE HAPPY.

IN THIS MOMENT, I CHOOSE TO BE JOYOUS.

IN THIS MOMENT, I CHOOSE TO BE PEACEFUL AND HOPEFUL.

IN THIS MOMENT, TIME IS NOT MINE TO GIVE OR TAKE BUT, TO USE OR FILL WITH HEALTHY ACTIVITY NOURISHING MYSELF AN OTHERS.

SUGGESTED MEETING TOPICS:

WE ARE WELL

DAILY WELLNESS WORKOUT

W.I.L.D. (WELLNESS IN LIFE DISCOVERY) VS.

RECOVERY

HOW WELL AM I?

HOW DO I SET GOALS?

MY PERSONAL TRIUMPHS

W.I.L.D TOOLS

Recovery Coaching Service of New York, LLC

Seven Dimensions of Wellness

Please rate using the following scale
Always (5), Very Frequently (4), Frequently (3), Occasionally (2), Almost Never (1), Never (0)

Physical Wellness

1. I exercise for 30 minutes or more most days of the week
   5 4 3 2 1 0
2. My exercise program includes activities that build my heart, muscles and flexibility

   5 4 3 2 1 0
3. I select lean cuts of meat, poultry or fish
   5 4 3 2 1 0
4. I eat a variety of food from all the food groups
   5 4 3 2 1 0
5. I eat breakfast
   5 4 3 2 1 0
6. I get an adequate amount of sleep (7-8 hours per night)
   5 4 3 2 1 0
7. I examine my breasts or testes once a month
   5 4 3 2 1 0
8. I participate in recommended periodic health screenings (blood pressure, etc.)

   5 4 3 2 1 0
9. I seek medical advice when needed
   5 4 3 2 1 0
10. I drink less than 5 alcoholic drinks at a sitting
    5 4 3 2 1 0
11. I avoid drinking while under the influence of alcohol
    5 4 3 2 1 0
12. I avoid using tobacco products
    5 4 3 2 1 0

Environmental Wellness
1. I minimize my exposure to second hand tobacco smoke
   5 4 3 2 1 0
2. I keep my vehicle maintained to ensure safety
   5 4 3 2 1 0
3. When I see a safety hazard, I take steps to correct the problem

   5 4 3 2 1 0
4. I choose an environment that is free of excessive noise whenever possible

   5 4 3 2 1 0
5. I make efforts to reduce, reuse and recycle
   5 4 3 2 1 0
6. I try to create an environment that minimizes my stress
   5 4 3 2 1 0
7.

Spiritual Wellness
1. I make time for relaxation in my day
   5 4 3 2 1 0
2. I make time in my day for prayer, meditation or personal time   5 4 3 2 1 0
3. My values guide my actions and decisions
   5 4 3 2 1 0
4. I am accepting of the views of others
   5 4 3 2 1 0

Emotional/Psychological Wellness
1. I am able to sleep soundly throughout the night and wake feeling refreshed

   5 4 3 2 1 0
2. I am able to make decisions with a minimum of stress and worry
   5 4 3 2 1 0
3. I am able to set priorities
   5 4 3 2 1 0
4. I maintain a balance between school, work and personal life
   5 4 3 2 1 0

Intellectual Wellness
1. It is easy for me to apply knowledge from one situation to another
   5 4 3 2 1 0
2. I enjoy the amount and variety I read
   5 4 3 2 1 0
3. I find life intellectually challenging and stimulating
   5 4 3 2 1 0

85

4. I obtain health information from reputable sources
    5 4 3 2 1 0
5. I spend money commensurate with my income, values, and goals
    5 4 3 2 1 0
6. I pay my bills in full each month (including my credit card)
    5 4 3 2 1 0

Occupational Wellness

1. I am able to plan a manageable workload
    5 4 3 2 1 0
2. My career is consistent with my values and goals
    5 4 3 2 1 0
3. I earn enough money to meet my needs to provide stability for me and/or my family

    5 4 3 2 1 0
4. My work benefits individuals and/or society
    5 4 3 2 1 0

Social Wellness

1. I plan time to be with my family and friends
    5 4 3 2 1 0
2. I enjoy my time with others
    5 4 3 2 1 0
3. I am satisfied with the groups/organizations that I am part of

    5 4 3 2 1 0
4. My relationships with others are positive and rewarding
    5 4 3 2 1 0
5. I explore diversity by interacting with people of other cultures, background, and beliefs
    5 4 3 2 1 0

STAGES OF CHANGE

- In treatment or out of treatment change occurs in stages (see below and H-2.0).

Stage of Change	Characteristics
1. Pre-contemplation	Not currently considering change: "Ignorance is bliss".
2. Contemplation	Ambivalent about change: "Sitting on the fence". Not considering change in the next month.
3. Preparation	Some experience trying to change: "Testing the waters". Planning to act within 1month.
4. Action	Practicing new behavior. 3-6 months.
5. Maintenance	Continued commitment to sustaining new behavior. 6 months - 5 years
6. Relapse	Return to old behaviors:

PROS AND CONS OF CHANGING AND OF STAYING THE SAME

- Motivation provides you with a <u>reason</u> to act in a certain way.

- Motivation is influenced by how you view <u>what you will gain</u> and <u>what you will lose</u> by acting in different ways.

- Most things you do have good and not-so-good things about them. This may cause you to have mixed feelings, or <u>ambivalence</u>, about changing some of your actions.

- When you are ambivalent you have a harder time making decisions because nothing you do will meet <u>all</u> of your needs.

- It helps to look at both sides at the same time, the good and not-so-good.

- Work on the "Decisional Balance" worksheet (W-5.0) to understand better all sides of changing and not changing.

<u>Recovery Coaching Service of New York, LLC</u>
Weekly Contingency Management Plan

Recoveree's Name:
_____   Date of Plan:
_____

Recovery Coach:
_____

Date of next planning meeting to review this plan: _____

The first activity or step related to my long-term goal of :
_____

The first step or activity that I would like to accomplish is:
_____

_____
_____

When I accomplish this step or activity I will receive:
_____

_____
_____

Confirmation of this step or activity will include:
_____

_____
_____

To accomplish this step or activity I will receive assistance from (describe who and what the assistance will be):
_____
_____

The second activity or step related to my long-term goal of:

_____

The second step or activity that I would like to accomplish is:

_____

_____

_____

When I accomplish this step or activity I will receive:

_____

_____

_____

Confirmation of this step or activity will include:

_____

_____

_____

To accomplish this step or activity I will receive assistance from (describe who and what the assistance will be):

_____

_____

ABOUT THE AUTHOR

Lucious Conway (1963 -) was born in River Rouge, Michigan, to African American and Native American parents. For more than twenty-five years he worked as a paralegal across the country as well as produced and hosted talk radio programs in New York, Washington, D.C., Detroit, and Florida. He is a stage, television and film actor, writer and producer. His first audio book was published in 2004 entitled "Happy Hour." He is divorced and now lives alone in New York City. Lucious is the founder and owner of New York States' first and only peer run company certified to bill Medicaid directly and under contract to an insurance company (UnitedHealthcare/Optum) as a provider of Peer Support and Bridger Services. His company Recovery Coaching Service of New York, LLC remains the only one in the world with a private insurance and Medicaid/Medicare approved and certified method of peer non clinical S.O.A.P. notation for reimbursement.

For more information contact Lucious at:
347.454.4492
New York, NY
rcsnewyork@gmail.com

CPSIA information can be obtained
at www.ICGtesting.com
Printed in the USA
LVHW012322260523
748152LV00002B/50